CONTENTS

Copyright
Foreword
The RED bridge   4
The ORANGE bridge   10
The YELLOW bridge   17
The GREEN bridge   23
The BLUE bridge   30
The INDIGO bridge   38
The PURPLE bridge   48
Glossary   56
Summary of our chakras   58
Meditation   62
About The Author   66
Books By This Author   68
Books By This Author   70

Copyright © 2022 Diana White

All rights reserved

The characters and events portrayed in this book are fictitious. Any similarity to real persons, living or dead, is coincidental and not intended by the author.

No part of this book may be reproduced, or stored in a retrieval system, or transmitted in any form or by any means, electronic, mechanical, photocopying, recording, or otherwise, without express written permission of the publisher.

ISBN: 9798842717590

Cover design and illustrations by: Diana White

FOREWORD

"What you will find on this journey may bring many answers to your questions, yet it's not necessarily what you seek."

Diana White

Crystal's journey over the rainbow

Introduction:

One day Crystal woke up and looked out of the window. Before her was this beautiful rainbow, spanning the whole width, as far as her eyes could see.

The rainbow colours were glorious, vivid and bright. She wondered: 'What do all these colours mean and why are they there?' She also remembered someone saying that there was a pot of gold at the end of the rainbow.

Crystal found herself thinking:
'What if I could find out what the colours mean?
What if there really is gold at the end of the rainbow'?
What if I could walk over the rainbow to get to the pot of gold?'

She decided to find out and closed her eyes.

Crystal was transported to the beginning of the rainbow and greeted by a guard who stood in front of a tall ornate golden gate.

The guard was dressed in a rainbow coloured cloak and held a golden staff in his hand.

The guard asked Crystal why she decided to come to the rainbow.

Crystal quickly said: "I want to find out what the colours mean and if there really is a pot of gold at the end of the rainbow?"

The guard laughed and said: "Everyone who came here before you has had the same questions."

Crystal asked: "Did they find out?"

The guard was silent for a while and smiled at her.

Eventually he said:
"Seeking the answers to your questions takes great commitment. A long and difficult journey lies ahead of you. What you will find on your journey may bring many answers to your questions yet it's not necessarily what you seek.

Many people before you did not want to enter into this commitment and went back home. However, for those of you who are prepared to take this journey, the rewards will be multiple.

Each colour of the rainbow represents a separate journey and question you must seek the answer to. Nobody can solve this for you but yourself."

Crystal understood. She knew this would not be easy and many challenges lay ahead.

Little did she know how this journey would affect her

whole life.

Crystal nodded and said to the rainbow guard:

"I'm ready."

And with that the guard opened the golden gate for her, smiled, and wished her much love and success.

THE RED BRIDGE

Crystal found herself stepping onto a red bridge. She was immediately enveloped by a bright red fog, completely blinding her.

She felt a little worried as she couldn't see anything at all. Then she noticed she was barefoot, her shoes had vanished! Out of the soles of her feet roots were forming, pulling her down into the ground she was standing on. Crystal suddenly found herself stuck and unable to move.

She sighed.

The rainbow guard appeared and smiled at her.

Crystal asked: "Why am I stuck when I'm supposed to be on a journey?"

The rainbow guard smiled and said:" Let me explain...

"The colour red represents our roots, our foundation.
If they are deep we don't wobble, yet if they're not we may find ourselves a little scattered.
Deep roots provide us with a good source of energy and nourishment, just like the trees receive theirs using their root system. They provide us with a solid foundation, platform and support, and they enable us to go with the flow of life.
Deep roots also allow us to release anything we need to let go of such as: old ideas, emotions, insecurities, perfectionism or patterns which no longer work for us.
This bridge is a new beginning for you.
To be able to cross this bridge you must grow deep roots and let go of what no longer serves you, so you can become who you really are."

And with that the rainbow guard vanished.
Crystal shouted after him: "But you didn't give me any instructions how I do that!"

Crystal was totally confused and just stood there.
How on earth could she grow deep roots and become who she really is when she knows exactly who she is.
Or does she?
And what is that about letting go of what no longer serves her?
She is perfectly happy as she is.
Or is she?

She suddenly realised the red fog had lifted, she was wearing her shoes again, and there was a red path in front of her. Crystal got a glimpse of an object on the

path and started walking. It looked like a treasure chest covered in beautiful shimmering gemstones. As she got closer to the treasure chest she became really excited about its content and started thinking about the pot of gold at the end of the rainbow.
Was it actually in this chest?

The treasure chest was indeed covered in beautiful gemstones of all colours. Crystal crouched down to open the chest and as it opened her face dropped.
It was empty!
Crystal looked confused and started to wonder if she had missed something entirely?
Why was the chest empty?

Out of nowhere a voice appeared and said: "You must fill this chest with everything you need to let go of that hinders you from being yourself."
Once again silence returned.

Crystal now understood what the rainbow guard meant by 'a long and difficult journey' and 'commitment'. It wouldn't be a race to the finish line.

Sat in front of the treasure chest Crystal started to cry, getting angry with herself. What had she let herself in for? All she wanted to do was to find out what the colours of the rainbow mean and if there really is a pot of gold at the end of it.

A mirror appeared in front of her. As she looked into it she could see herself in her current life. It was playing like a movie. She saw the house she lived in, her friends, her family, the things she enjoyed and didn't enjoy too.

It was telling her to reflect on who she really is and what she wants to do with her life.
Is what she is doing now really serving her?
A piece of paper and pen appeared.
She started writing.
She knew now upon reflection what she needed to change, let go of and bring into her life, so she could be who she wants to be: herself.

Once she had written everything down Crystal placed the piece of paper into the chest and closed it.
The chest vanished.
Crystal had made her first commitment to herself by creating a new beginning to be the authentic self that she is. This will provide her with solid foundations for her life's journey.

Advice from Crystal:

In life we can get so wrapped up in our fears, insecurities, social pressure, gossip, outdated ideas and so on, that we forget we are an individual. Everyone of us is unique and what works for one doesn't necessarily work for another.

Follow your true self and be authentic.

Crystal encourages you to practise this self-reflection exercise:
Find a quiet space and write down how you can make changes in your life to get back to your authentic self.
Who are you really?
What are your likes and dislikes?
Where are you giving your power, your energy, away?

THE ORANGE BRIDGE

Crystal now found herself standing on an orange bridge. A misty orange colour was enveloping her and almost pushed her forward, towards something. An angel suddenly appeared by her side. She had never seen something so beautiful before and Crystal was mesmerised.

The angel guided her towards a castle. It was not your usual castle with turrets nor was it inviting. A plank appeared inviting Crystal to step onto it. And without any warning she was caged it. Trapped again.

She was behind bars surrounded on all four sides. Beneath her was a flowing river, the water gushing very fast almost in a hurry to get somewhere.

Crystal panicked and her mind was whirling with thoughts of drowning if the plank she was standing on collapses.

The rainbow guard appeared beside her and Crystal felt almost relieved. He could help her escape this cage.

She asked the guard: "How can I get out of here?"

The rainbow guard smiled and said:

"The colour orange refers to our emotions. Often our emotions keep holding us hostage and we carry them all. To free yourself you must first discover the child within."

And with that he was gone.

Crystal felt helpless. How would she manage to free herself from this prison?
The angel she saw earlier reappeared by her side.
"Let's fly", the angel said.
Taken by her hand, Crystal found herself lifted off her feet and zoomed up in the air.
With the wind in her face she started to smile and feel the freedom of being able to fly like a bird, no fear of falling.
She could see the orange bridge beneath her, the cage she left behind and the castle next to it.

The castle was glowing in a vivid orange colour and projected all the things she loved as a child. There was no worry what the day would bring. She felt free, free as a bird. She loved that feeling.

The angel took her into the castle grounds and disappeared.

Crystal slowly took a look around. The entrance door to the castle shimmered and caught her eyes.
Another treasure chest stood right in front of the entrance. Remembering that the last chest was empty Crystal almost sighed as she tried to open it.

To her surprise she found a clear crystal ball in it. Now intrigued, she picked it up and gazed into it. She could see different faces showing different emotions. Crystal could relate to all of them.
Then her own face appeared and started talking to her.
It said: "How you deal with your emotions on a daily basis is a true reflection of what you carry each day. Are you letting people walk over you, your mind run away with you or are you in charge? Please reflect on this."

The rainbow guard reappeared by her side and offered her three keys to choose from but only one key would open the castle door to the next bridge. He vanished again.
As they all looked identical, it would be the luck of the draw which one would fit.

Crystal stood in front of the castle door. She put in the first key and to her surprise the door opened straight away. She walked through the door smiling to herself and entered a room. The door closed behind her and the room started to fill with water.
Crystal started to panic and looked around to find a way out but to her surprise all doors and windows had

vanished.

The water was now up to her waist. Soon it would be up to her neck and she got more and more frightened. A voice suddenly said: "Our emotions can feel like they're drowning us but we have a choice of how we react and deal with them."

Crystal suddenly remembered the plank she stood on when she was caged in and the angel that took her flying. She now understood that she can rise above her emotions, see them from a different perspective, and share them with her support network of loved ones whenever she needed to free herself from the constraints.

The water drained and a door appeared in the wall of the room she was standing in.

She opened the door with another key and stepped into the next room. It was dark and eerie. Suddenly faces appeared of people she knew and those she didn't. All of them where talking to her at the same time, telling her what to do and making decisions for her. She could feel the immense pressure on her body. The pressure felt almost overwhelming, her body aching, her stomach turning and her head spinning.
Crystal was crouching down guarding herself.
She wanted everyone to stop.

"Why can't you just all stop", she shouted. But it carried on. It became unbearable.

The angel appeared by her side and said: "Remember

that everyone will have an opinion on everything and everyone will have a way of doing something. However it may not be how you choose to see or do things in your life."

Crystal remembered the cage she was trapped in before, standing on the plank above the water. She imagined herself back in this cage and with that the noise stopped. She now understood that the cage was her protection from other people's opinions and pressures and not a prison, to allow her to make the correct choices and decisions for herself. She values her self-worth.

The room she stood in was now light and bright and a new door appeared. She put in the last key and opened the door. A yellow bridge appeared before her eyes.
She knew the next bridge awaits.

Advice from Crystal:

No matter what people say or do please respect your selfworth. You do not have to feel guilty of saying NO or cancelling appointments. Trust yourself to make the right decisions at the right time. And most of all, don't get caught up in all the emotions and let them run away with you. Stop, breathe, observe and see the bigger picture.

Think of a time when you were really emotionally challenged. What are your emotional patterns and how could you improve on that?

THE YELLOW BRIDGE

Crystal found herself in the midst of a sunflower field. She loves sunflowers, they are her favourite. They feel like a ray of sunshine to her; always happy, always smiling.

One of the sunflowers turned to her and spoke: "What brings you true happiness Crystal?"

Crystal stood for a moment and started to think. Her thoughts were taking her to all sorts of places, experiences and things she has and doesn't have. Her mind was whirling so much it started to make her feel dizzy and off-balance. She was torn between so many things that could make her happy.

The rainbow guard appeared next to her and smiled. "Beautiful sunflowers", he said.
"Come with me Crystal, I want to show you something." And with that they were swept off their feet and hovered over a vast field of sunflowers.

The rainbow guard spoke:

"The colour yellow refers to our thought process, instincts, fears and choices. Can you see all these sunflowers and how far they stretch? Imagine this is your mind Crystal; all the thoughts we are collecting, processing and dealing with. How can we truly decide what makes us happy with all this going on in our mind?"

Suddenly Crystal found herself back next to the sunflower that spoke to her earlier. A small clearing had appeared and she could see a bench. She walked over to it and sat down.
"Do you believe in miracles?" a voice asked. Crystal noticed the angel sitting beside her. "I don't know", Crystal answered truthfully. "Well", said the angel, "then you'll just have to trust.
I'd like you to think of something that weighs heavily on your mind and you've been thinking about for a while on how to resolve this issue. Write it down on a piece of paper and then put it in this little box."
The box was only small and had white fluffy feathers on top.

Crystal could think of a few things she would want a solution for. She decided on one and started writing it down. As she was writing it down Crystal could sense the emotions that came with this thought, the heaviness in her stomach and on her shoulders.

She finished writing and folded up the piece of paper then placed it in the box and closed the lid.

The angel reappeared and said: "Now take the box to the sunflower you spoke to earlier and ask it if you can make a wish."

Crystal thought: 'It's all a bit odd and what could a sunflower do with her wish?'

Reluctantly she walked over to the sunflower and said: "The angel has asked me if I could make a wish."

The sunflower nodded and asked what was in the box she was holding. Crystal mentioned it was a problem she would like a solution to.

The sunflower said: "I'd like you to visualise how you would solve this problem until you feel the happiness in your belly, then place the box on the ground in front of me."

Crystal thought: 'Oh well I will give it a try.'

Crystal closed her eyes. The emotions relating to her problem came back into her body. She didn't like that feeling. She started to think of solutions and tried to visualise it in her minds eye. 'Oh it's difficult', she thought.

The angel whispered in her ear: "Trust."

Crystal realised she had to go with her instincts on what she felt was the right thing to do.

Now she had visualised that outcome and noticed the

happy feeling in her stomach she placed the box beneath the sunflower.

The box vanished.

Crystal felt some sense of relief and wondered what had happened.

She noticed the sunflowers parting to reveal a path. She started to walk, almost skipping. She smiled to herself.

A door appeared at the end of the path with a sign saying: 'I trust myself to make the correct choices'

Crystal opened the door and stepped onto the green bridge.

Advice from Crystal:

Crystal had realised that the key to true happiness was within her all the time.

A scattered mind can take away from making the right choices and decisions yet if we trust our instincts it's so much easier. Sometimes this also means making a tough decision and taking a leap of faith, not knowing what the outcome will be.

Trust yourself more.

THE GREEN BRIDGE

Crystal thought to herself that this journey certainly isn't easy, however she has learned so much already.
Nothing however could prepare her of what she would be facing next.
She suddenly felt surrounded by a deep slimy green substance. It was sticky and not at all pleasant. Crystal took a look around and realised it was a lake of green slime she was standing in.
'Great!', she thought to herself, 'How am I going to get out of this?'
Waist-deep stuck in this green lake she tried to move herself forward, out of this grim place.
The angel suddenly appeared hovering above her and said: "Deep down in this lake is a gem you will need to find to free yourself." The angel vanished as quickly as it had appeared.
Crystal was now angry. Bashing her hands into the slimy green stuff she shouted out loud: "I've had enough! Take me home!"
The rainbow guard appeared by her side and said:

"The colour green represents our heart. You must delve deep into the depths of your own heart to unlock this jewel."

Crystal shook her head and started crying. "I can't do it, I hate slime. I hate being constantly trapped.", she said.
By that time the rainbow guard had gone.

Finding herself alone in a slimy green lake is not what she had asked for.
Pulling herself together a bit Crystal took a few deep breaths and then remembered the words of the angel and the rainbow guard. She had a closer look around as to how she could get to the gem she was asked to find. Crystal scanned the lake and its surroundings looking for clues and tools that may enable her to do this after all.

There was NOTHING, absolutely nothing.

'Think again Crystal', she said to herself.

A white horse appeared by the edge of the lake. It was so

beautiful and almost magical. It shimmered in the light. Crystal suddenly noticed it bowed to her and showed itself in its full glory. It was a unicorn.
It tipped its horn into the green slimy lake and the lake transformed into a whirlpool of sparkling rainbow colours.
The centre of the lake started to part and it revealed a red heart-shaped crystal lying at the bottom of it.
Crystal was mesmerised yet also extremely happy that she now knew what gem was awaiting her.
The unicorn stepped back, vanished, and in a flash the lake had transformed back to what it was before: green and slimy.

Crystal was so disappointed. She was so close yet so far from retrieving the red heart-shaped gem at the bottom of the lake.

'There must be a trick to this', she thought.
How could she transform this lake to be able to get to the gem?

She started thinking and thinking and thinking some more.
Somehow she remembered the words she had heard before: "Trust yourself."

Crystal closed her eyes and started to imagine that the lake had transformed into a rainbow coloured whirlpool before her, just like the unicorn had done.

She opened one eye just to check. To her disappointment nothing had changed.
The angel returned by her side and asked: "What are you

doing?"
Crystal told the angel the story of the unicorn and the angel started laughing.
Now Crystal was annoyed and crossed her arms over her chest. She was sulking.
The angel then said: "It's all within you Crystal, open your heart."

Crystal found herself alone again. This so far has been the most difficult task.
She still hasn't got a clue of how to get to the gem and all the angel could do was laugh at her. 'How rude', she thought.

On the other hand if she wants to get out of this she'll have to come up with a solution fast.
The angels voice reappeared, repeating its words: "It's all within you Crystal, open your heart."

'Open my heart', Crystal thought to herself. 'How am I going to do that?'

Suddenly in front of her this little bird had appeared, clearly fallen into the lake and struggling. From the noise it made it became clear it was drowning. Surrounded by all the green slime its feathers became glued together and there was no escape.

Crystal pushed herself forward to help this poor little bird, trying to rescue it from drowning. She picked it up and held it close to her chest, wiping off the green slime from its feathers as best as she could.
She cradled it in her arms and thought of how she would love a warming hug right now herself.

The little bird was now calm and comfortable in her arms and in return Crystal started to feel comforted herself.
Crystal now realised that she had saved this little bird's life and stopped it from drowning. She felt good about herself.
What she hadn't noticed was that she no longer stood in a green slimy lake.
She was back on the green bridge still caring for this young bird she had rescued, completely unaware of her surroundings.

The angel reappeared in front of her and said: "Well done Crystal you did it."
Only now had she realised that she was back on the bridge.
The angel smiled at her and said: "The key to solving this was always in your heart. When you follow your heart true miracles happen."

Crystal felt so relieved and satisfied with herself. She handed the little bird to the angel to help it fly again. They vanished.
A new door appeared in front of her, Crystal opened it and stepped through.

Advice from Crystal:

Our heart holds our true wisdom. You can trick yourself into knowing exactly what to do yet if we truly open our heart to receive we have a deep inner knowing of what we really need to do.
True love heals our wounds and those of others.
Love unconditionally without any agenda and what you receive in return will be true miracles.

THE BLUE BRIDGE

'That was a tough one', Crystal thought to herself. 'The more bridges I climb the harder it seems to get.'
Could she handle more to get to the end of the rainbow and find that pot of gold?

The rainbow guard appeared and said: "Walk with me Crystal." Both started walking in complete silence. Crystal desperately wanted to speak yet felt it would interrupt and potentially offend the rainbow guard. So they continued on the blue bridge in silence.

Crystal felt so uncomfortable to the point whereby it became unbearable. She needed to say something. So she decided to ask the rainbow guard: "Where are we going?"

The rainbow guard kept silent. 'Odd, very odd', thought Crystal. They kept walking.
As Crystal had been through a few challenges by now she started to think to herself that this may be a lesson too.

The rainbow guard would normally say something even though it may not make sense to her.

Eventually they had reached a tall standing mirror.
The rainbow guard said:

"The colour blue represents our communication with ourself and others. The way we express ourselves is a true reflection of who we are".
With that he left.

Crystal now stood in front of the tall mirror, looking at herself, wondering what to do with it. She walked around the mirror and even touched it to see if anything would happen.

The angel had appeared and stood in front of the mirror and spoke: "Mirror, mirror show me now." A bright blinding golden-white light beamed out of it enveloping the angel and everything in its surroundings.
Crystal was taken aback and completely astounded. 'Wow', she thought. Her mouth was wide open.

The golden-white light faded and the angel said to Crystal: "Now you give it a try."
Excited to give it a go Crystal stood herself in front of the mirror and said:" Mirror, mirror show me now."
Expecting to repeat what the angel had done Crystal

waited but to her disappointment all she could see was a reflection of herself in the mirror.
She turned to the angel to ask how it was done but yet again the angel had disappeared.

'Ok', she thought, 'Maybe I didn't speak clearly and loud enough?' So she tried again and said: "Mirror, mirror show me now."
Crystal stood and waited. Again nothing!

"I don't understand the point of this", she said to the mirror and sat down in front of it.
The mirror suddenly spoke and said: "So you give up that easily? What is the one thing you are really passionate about and want the world to know?"

Crystal was a little upset with herself that she had given up so easily again.
'What am I really passionate about and want to share with the world?', she asked herself.

All sorts of thoughts came to her mind as she sat there contemplating. Nobody had ever asked her this question before so how could she know the answer to that?

Crystal started pacing up and down in front of the mirror completely consumed by her thoughts.

The mirror interrupts her: "Have you thought about something?"
"Maybe", Crystal said; yet she wasn't sure.
"Let's try", said the mirror.

Crystal stood in front of the mirror, with her thought on her mind and said: "Mirror, mirror show me now."

A tiny speckle of light flashed but vanished as quickly as it appeared.
"What happened?", she asked the mirror.
"You can do better than that", it said.

'Back to the drawing board', Crystal thought. This is hard, harder than she imagined.

Hours must have gone by and Crystal was still contemplating.
The rainbow guard appeared by her side again and said: "Crystal, remember to speak with truth and conviction. If you want to be heard you must live it".

With that on her mind she found herself alone again in front of the mirror.
'But what if nobody cares or wants to hear what I've got to say?', she suddenly thought. Doubts were creeping in.
The mirror spoke to Crystal and said: "What if nobody could hear you but yourself? What would you say?"

Finally, after what seemed an eternity, Crystal stood up and looked into the mirror. She looked at herself and said: "Mirror, mirror show me now." Again a speckle of light flashed out of the mirror and vanished.

"Louder", a voice said.

Crystal repeated the words with a bit more vitality: "Mirror, mirror show me now."
This time she noticed that the light coming out of the mirror was bigger and brighter for a bit longer before it vanished again.
"Mean it", a voice said.

Crystal almost shouted: "Mirror, mirror show me now."
The light grew even bigger and brighter and glowed for even longer.
Crystal was now so much more upbeat and decided to try once more. With the thought firmly in her head she wanted to give it one last try.

So she gathered all her inner strength determined to succeed this time.
Crystal said loud and clear: "Mirror, mirror show me now."

A beam of golden-white light went straight into her heart and then poured out of her, enveloping her whole body and her surroundings.

Crystal was once again mesmerised by the light and so happy she had finally achieved what the angel had showed her.
The light slowly faded and the angel was by her side, smiling at her.

Crystal started jumping up and down said: "I did it, I did it, I did it".
The angel spoke: "Crystal, what you haven't realised yet is that the beam of light in the mirror is a reflection of yourself. Only when you express your true self your light will shine and capture everyone."

Crystal now understood that once again 'it's all within herself', a lesson she was taught over and over again.

She noticed the mirror had now vanished and the blue bridge was coming to the end.

A mystical looking door had appeared she wasn't sure she wanted to open.
Crystal knew she had to do it to be able to continue on her journey.

Advice from Crystal:

The way we communicate with ourselves and others is a true reflection of who we are and of how we express ourselves and our actions.
We must take personal responsibility of speaking our truth from our heart and never question how it is received. Your message will reach those who need to hear it, in the correct way, at the exact right time.
Trust in your voice.

◆ ◆ ◆

THE INDIGO BRIDGE

As Crystal stepped onto the indigo bridge it was dark. All she could see was a few stars twinkling in the sky.
She felt uneasy and literally tiptoed forward, trying not to trip over something.
She could hear an owl, it swooped in and sat on a branch above her.

Crystal now managed to see outlines of trees as she continued tiptoeing forward. Branches crackled beneath her feet.
'This is creepy', she thought.

It seemed to get darker and darker to the point where Crystal was stretching her arms out to feel for things, as she couldn't see anymore.
The rainbow guard appeared with a lantern in his hand in front of her.
"Why is it so dark here?", Crystal asked him.
He replied:

"The colour indigo represents our inner vision. You must learn to see without sight."

He was gone and Crystal stood in complete darkness once more.
Sometimes she wished he'd stop speaking in riddles. And anyway what does it mean: "You must learn to see without sight. My eyes work perfectly fine."

Crystal isn't particularly fond of the dark and was finding it difficult to know which direction she needed to take. All she had to go by were the little twinkling stars in the sky but they didn't provide enough light at all.

Something caught her eyes though. A twinkling different from the stars. It almost seemed like a reflection of some sort. She slowly tried to move towards that twinkling and came to a small table. In the middle of the table stood a crystal ball which was creating the twinkling she noticed earlier.
It was reflecting light but she couldn't see where from.

Crystal sat herself on the stool in front of the table and

gazed into the crystal ball. A bright light was dancing in it. It started forming a shape of something and as Crystal looked closer she noticed a little fairy fluttering around, as if it was dancing.
Intrigued Crystal kept watching this fairy.
The fairy didn't seem to notice her at all. 'Could she see me?', Crystal wondered.
She tapped on the crystal ball to check if it would get the fairy's attention but she quickly realised that it didn't. It seemed like a completely different world in there.

Crystal was interrupted by the angel who now stood by her side. "Can you see it?", the angel asked.
"The fairy you mean?", Crystal replied.
"No", said the angel.
"See what?", Crystal asked.
"The inner world", the angel replied.

She took a closer look at the crystal ball. The world inside seemed familiar yet not.
Crystal was certainly intrigued but didn't understand what the angel meant by 'inner world'.

The rainbow guard appeared and said to Crystal: "We have two eyes to look and one to see. When we see clearly we have a true knowing we cannot explain. We simply know."

Crystal was somewhat bemused about this as well as curious. 'How could we have two eyes to see and only one to look?', she wondered.

Facing the crystal ball again she noticed something odd. The crystal ball appeared to have become larger. 'How's

this possible?', she thought.
Crystal gazed into it and noticed the fairy had disappeared. In fact everything had disappeared. All she could see now was the reflection of her face.
"Very mysterious", Crystal said to herself.

The moon had risen and was now glowing beautifully in the sky. Crystal has always been in awe of it yet couldn't explain why.
People have questioned many times whether there's a man living on the moon, lighting up his lantern to shine it down to us so we can see where we are going.

Crystal's thoughts were suddenly interrupted by a fluttering. The owl she saw earlier was now sat on the table in front of her, next to the crystal ball.

The owl stared at her and Crystal wasn't entirely sure what to make of it. She noticed though that the owl could turn its head right around to look behind. Owls can see exceptionally well in the dark and very far too.
'Imagine we could do this? We could see absolutely everything.', she thought.

Crystal now noticed that the owl had what seemed like a necklace and a blue gem attached to it. 'Oh, what's this?' Crystal thought.

She slowly moved her hand towards the owl to reach the gem and as she did the owl flew off and the gem tumbled onto the table. Crystal noticed it was a deep dark blue colour and as she picked it up she suddenly had some strange visions in her head.

Crystal threw the gem quickly back on the table. "Now that was weird", she said to herself.
"What was that?
How can a gem do this?"

She wasn't sure what to do next but at the same time she was still intrigued.

The rainbow guard now stood beside her and said: "I see you've got hold of the gemstone."
"What does it do?", Crystal asked.
"It will help you see until you can see yourself.", the rainbow guard replied.
Crystal looked at him confused.
"But I can see with my eyes", she said.

As in normal fashion the rainbow guard vanished and left Crystal to figure it out for herself.

Crystal knew this was another lesson for her so she had to be brave and trust him.
She tentatively picked up the dark blue gemstone again and strange images flashed before her eyes.

Nothing she could make out with any meaning or detail at all. It seemed all blurred and jumbled up.
She put the gemstone down again. Crystal honestly didn't know what to make of this.
Nothing made sense. She certainly didn't understand what this gemstone was for and how it was going to help her see.

The angel appeared by her side and said: "Why don't you try putting the blue gemstone on your forehead?", and vanished.

'Ok', Crystal thought, 'let's try'.
She took the gemstone into her hand and held it to her forehead. Crystal closed her eyes.
What happened next was truly magical.

Crystal started to see colours in her mind's eye, floating and creating beautiful shapes. It was like looking through a kaleidoscope. She couldn't get enough of it.
With a sudden jolt through her body Crystal was transported back to reality.

She felt a little strange but couldn't put her finger on as to why.

The rainbow guard had reappeared and smiled. "What did you see?", he asked.
"Beautiful colours", Crystal managed to say.

"I told you it would help you see", the rainbow guard said. He continued: "Now to truly see you must rely on your own inner guidance and intuition without questioning. We call it our inner navigation system to help us make the correct choices in life.
To find the next door you must solely rely on it."

Crystal noticed everything around her had vanished and she stood in total darkness. No moon, no stars, no owl, no nothing.
Even the gemstone had gone.

Crystal could only think of the beautiful colours she had seen. She closed her eyes but nothing happened. No colours, no strange blurred visions.

She knew she had to find the next door yet she didn't know how to.

As before she tiptoed forward not knowing whether she even went in the right direction or where she was heading to. It felt eerie, totally silent and simply creepy.

What Crystal hadn't realised yet was that she found herself standing in the crystal ball she had gazed into at the beginning.

The rainbow guard, the angel and the owl were sat in front of the crystal ball watching her.

The only way out for her was to imagine and see the colours of the rainbow in front of her to light up the path to the next door.

The crystal ball around her was for protection to keep her safe.

A voice so strong inside of Crystal's mind kept repeatedly saying:
' light up the path to the next door with rainbow colours'
' light up the path to the next door with rainbow colours'
' light up the path to the next door with rainbow colours'

Crystal couldn't ignore it and put all her focus into imagining the path in front of her being illuminated by the rainbow colours to guide her to the next door.

She closed her eyes and started imagining the colours. First red, then orange, then yellow, green, blue, indigo and lastly purple.

After a while she could clearly see them in her mind's eye and started walking forward. A vivid bright purple door appeared in the distance.

Crystal continued walking towards it, being watched over by the rainbow guard, angel and owl outside of the crystal ball.

She finally reached the purple door, beautifully decorated with purple gemstones.

Crystal paused to touch them.

Suddenly feeling a little uneasy she wondered if she was being watched and looked up. She saw the rainbow guard, the angel and the owl looking at her from outside a domed clear ceiling. She now realised she was standing in the crystal ball.

She felt tricked!

The rainbow guard had appeared by her side and said: "Well done Crystal, you followed your intuition and created a rainbow path to guide you to the next door."

He opened the vivid purple door and a bright light appeared, almost blinding Crystal.

"Your next bridge awaits", he said.

Advice from Crystal:

Our inner guidance, knowledge and wisdom may be a mystery to us yet when used correctly it can help us make the right decisions in life. How often have you felt you needed to do something important but didn't know why? How often have you changed directions because something inside you told you to? How often did you know something but you don't know how or why you knew?

We call it our sixth' sense. We all have it yet underutilise it by overthinking and questioning ourselves constantly. Through meditation and visualisation techniques we're able to access our inner navigation system better.

◆ ◆ ◆

THE PURPLE BRIDGE

As Crystal stepped up onto the purple bridge the light was absolutely blinding. She had not seen anything so bright before yet it felt very warm and calming.
With her hands held in front of her eyes she could just make out a path right in front of her feet.
As Crystal looked down she suddenly noticed she looked different. Her clothes had taken on every colour of the rainbow she had been through, except purple.

She was in awe.
'How is this possible?', Crystal thought.
'Or is it another test?'

The intense bright light had faded by now and Crystal found herself surrounded by a golden sparkly light.
It was shimmering beautifully like sunlight yet there was something different about it. She couldn't put her finger on it.

Crystal started walking to explore her surroundings. Unlike the other bridges this one seemed totally different, but how?

Why couldn't she figure it out?
Why had her clothes changed colours to reflect the bridges she had completed?

It all seemed a mystery.
Something dawned on Crystal she had completely forgotten: the pot of gold at the end of the rainbow!
Was this it?
Could she really have found it?

Crystal suddenly felt really excited about the possibility she had managed to do what others haven't: She actually got to the end of the rainbow and found the pot of gold. She smiled to herself.

The rainbow guard had appeared and shook Crystal out of her thoughts:

"You've done very well Crystal. Be proud of yourself. You've learned many lessons yet there is one final one to complete. This one however will by far be the most transformative you must entirely complete by yourself. The colour purple refers to our consciousness and enlightenment. Only when you have found the light will you be complete."

And with that the rainbow guard had left again.

'Find the light', Crystal thought. 'What on earth could that mean?'

"I'm already surrounded by light", she said to herself.

Crystal turned around to find out what this light she was supposed to find was all about. A huge mirror stood in front of her.
It showed Crystal in her new and almost rainbow coloured clothes. The mirror then started to show her images of her and the lessons she had learned on the other bridges.
The red bridge and roots growing out of her feet.
The orange bridge and being trapped behind bars, stood on a plank over the river.
The yellow bridge and the sunflowers, holding a box with a solution to a problem.
The green bridge and the slimy lake she had to find a gemstone in.
The blue bridge and the mirror that was shining the light back at her.
And finally the indigo bridge and the crystal ball she found herself in.

'It's been one tough journey', Crystal thought.
'All these challenges just for a pot of gold.'

The mirror was now reflecting the golden sparkly light that was all around her.
"Is this the light I'm supposed to find?", she asked the mirror.

The mirror continued to pour the golden sparkly light

out.

Crystal remembered what she did on the blue bridge and thought it was worth a try.

She said to the mirror: "Mirror, mirror, show me now."
The mirror continued to show her the golden sparkly light.

Crystal knew it wasn't working yet this time she was determined not to give up so easily, considering she was totally on her own now.

She turned back to the mirror and noticed it was now showing her the rainbow guard, the angel, the unicorn, the fairy, the owl and all the gemstones she had encountered on her journey over the rainbow.

Crystal suddenly started to question why they were there in the first place. Were they helping her on her journey or causing all the trouble?
Are they actually real?

Her mind was whirling with all these questions.

Determined to carry on Crystal faced the mirror again only to notice that the mirror was now showing the purple path continuing in it.
Crystal wasn't sure what to make of this yet intrigued she walked towards the mirror and decided to touch it.

Her hand pushed through the mirror.
She quickly pulled it out again and gasped: "What was that!"
Crystal took a look at her hand to check it and to her amazement it was still fully intact.

Now slightly scared she wondered if the mirror was some kind of portal to another world or if it's another trick or lesson.
She wasn't sure what to do.
Should she try again or walk away?

After what seemed like an eternity Crystal decided to try again.
'What's the worst thing that could happen?', she thought.

She slowly reached into the mirror, fingers and hand first, then stepped through.

Crystal found herself floating, light as a feather. It almost felt as if she was weightless and nothing mattered here.
She was surrounded by all the rainbow colours which seemed to carry and support here beautifully.

All Crystal could think of was that she can fly without wings, no fear of falling.
The rainbow colours enveloped her one by one: red, orange, yellow, green, blue, indigo and purple.

With each colour washing through her Crystal felt even more fantastic and light. 'She could stay here forever', she thought.

With that thought however she was transported back and found herself standing in front of the mirror again.
Crystal saw herself in the mirror and noticed that a golden sparkly light was shining above her head.
Had she finally found the light?

She also realised that her clothes now showed all the rainbow colours from red to purple.
Crystal herself had transformed into a rainbow.

The rainbow guard now stood by her side and handed her a golden staff. As Crystal touched it the light from on top of her head poured through her body and out through her heart.

Crystal had found the light.
She was the light.
She had always been the light.

She is Rainbow Crystal.

The rainbow guard smiled at her and Crystal smiled back. He took her by her hand and in a flash both were stood back at the entrance of the rainbow, where they had first met.
He nodded to Crystal and said: "It's now your turn to help others on their journey over the rainbow."
He vanished.

Advice from Crystal:

We need to realise that we can all find the pot of gold within ourselves if we do the work. It may not be an easy journey to find enlightenment, wisdom and purpose in our world. However we are never really alone and can seek support from our family and friends and receive spiritual guidance, if we truly listen.

The rainbow colours represent our chakras or energy centres, spanning along our entire spine. Every day experiences can have positive and negative influences on our chakras and wellbeing. To remain balanced and in good health it is essential we nurture our chakras daily. This can be as simple as taking a few minutes to breathe deeply or imagine the rainbow colours flowing through our body and around us.

We may choose to use crystals or go out in nature, sing, dance or draw.

Do something every day that fills your soul with sparkle, with light, and reduce the things which don't make you feel good or happy.

◆ ◆ ◆

GLOSSARY

Crystal: represents each and every one of us on our journey through life

Rainbow guard: a wise person

Angel: a spiritual helper/guide

Owl: a visionary to help us view things from a wider perspective

Unicorn: a gentle energy, reminding us to be gentle with ourselves

Fairy: the carefree child within us

Mirror: a reflection of our life or inner world/feelings

Gemstones: a healing aid

Cage/castle: a protective shield around us or within us

Crystal Ball: a portal into our inner world/vision

Flying: viewing things from a higher perspective

Keys: the tools we have within us to unlock old beliefs/views

Sunflower: our solar plexus chakra

Chest/Box: a place for hidden treasures within ourselves

Chakras: our energy centres

Green lake/slime: an over-emotional accumulation of

things/experiences we have created

Inner vision/world: trusting our instincts or spiritual gifts

Moon: our inner shadow side

Rainbow: our chakras

Golden light/pot of gold: divine energy/enlightenment

◆ ◆ ◆

SUMMARY OF OUR CHAKRAS

Colour Red: our root chakra

our foundation.

If our roots are deep we don't wobble, yet if they're not we may find ourselves a little scattered.

Deep roots provide us with a good source of energy and nourishment, just like the trees receive theirs using their root system. They provide us with a solid foundation, platform and support and they enable us to go with the flow of life.

Deep roots also allow us to release anything we need to let go of such as: old ideas, emotions, insecurities, perfectionism or patterns which no longer work for us.

Let go of what no longer serves you so you can become who you really are.

+ Located at the base of our spine
+ Words associated with this chakra: Grounding, Foundation, Source of Energy, Support, Beginnings, Root of old ideas/patterns//emotions

Colour Orange: our sacral chakra

our emotions.

Often our emotions/feelings keep holding us hostage and we carry them all. To free yourself you must first discover the child within.
+ Located behind the naval/lower abdomen
+ Words associated with this chakra: Emotions/feelings, belief, observe, passion, self-worth, guilt, perseverance, comfort zone, completion, service

Colour Yellow: our solar plexus chakra

our thought process, instincts, fears and choices. All the energy we are collecting, processing and dealing with. How can we truly decide what makes us happy?
+ Located in our upper abdominal area
+ Words associated with this chakra: thought process/what's on our mind, planning process, problem solving, instinct/trust, joy, miracle, power, enlightenment, abundance, choices

Colour Green: our heart chakra

our heart/unconditional love. You must delve deep into your own depths of your heart to unlock it to its true potential.
+ Located in the middle of our chest area
+ Words associated with this chakra: gossip, growth, grief, victim, wisdom, trickery, perception, love, prosperity, peace, healing, hope, harmony, denying your true gifts

Colour blue: our throat chakra

our communication with ourself and others. The way we express ourselves is a true reflection of who we are.

+ Located at our throat

+ Words associated with this chakra: communication, truth, expression, to be heard and understood, personal responsibility, reflection, quest

Colour indigo: our third eye chakra

our inner vision. You must learn to see without sight.

+ Located between our eyes in the centre of our forehead

+ Words associated with this chakra: seeing the unseen, learn to see without sight, guidance, intuition, knowledge, spirituality, inner child, mystery, dignity, karmic issues, faith, sixth sense, past/future

Colour purple: our crown chakra

our consciousness and enlightenment. Only when you have found the light will you be complete.

+ Located above our head

+ Words associated with this chakra: enlightenment, consciousness, purpose, wisdom, spirit, spirituality, outside physical body, holding space

◆ ◆ ◆

MEDITATION

As we close our eyes they become very heavy. We make ourselves comfortable and relax our body more and more as we prepare to go on a journey over the seven rainbow bridges.

We visualise ourselves standing in front of a big golden gate. It shines brightly in its golden colour and it is covered in sparkly gemstones of all colours. A tall man appears. He introduces himself as the rainbow guard. He invites us to step in front of the golden gate. We take a deep breath in and as we breathe out the golden gate opens and we step through it.

We are standing on the first bridge, the red bridge. As we look down we notice we are barefoot and then feel a pull at the bottom of our feet. Roots are forming. They travel down far far into our Earth, providing us with stability and strength. A red light travels up through our roots and fills our feet, legs and root chakra, transmuting everything we no longer need. We are now safe and grounded and can move forward onto the second bridge, the orange bridge.

As we step onto the bridge an orange light envelopes us, filling our sacral chakra with joy, happiness, vitality and creativity. We release everything to the orange light which no longer serves us. We remember how to thrive and express ourselves. As the orange light fades we notice another bridge, the yellow bridge and we step onto it. A vast field of sunflowers stands before us, filling us with its yellow sun-like light. It makes us smile and we feel strong and empowered. The yellow light transmutes our anxiety, worries, fears and anything else which no longer serves us. We are free to express our truth.

As the yellow light returns to the sunflowers we see another bridge, the green bridge.

We take a step onto it. A warm green light envelopes us like a blanket, making us feel hugged and loved. It flows into our heart, uplifting us, and removes everything which ways down heavy on us. We feel lighter and brighter and our heart is happy and content. We understand that love is the key to solve any problems and to invite harmony into our life. As the green light fades a new bridge becomes visible, the blue bridge.

We step onto the blue bridge. A mirror appears in front of us and as we gaze into it we see ourselves. A blue light flows out of the mirror and into our throat chakra. It transmutes all unspoken words and any energies which do not serve us. It encourages us to always speak our truth and be the person we truly are. The blue light fades back into the mirror and it vanishes. We can see the next bridge, the indigo bridge.

We step forward onto it. We are surrounded by night sky with twinkling stars. Our vision adjusts and our third eye is cleared from all imbalances in this indigo light. We can see clearly now, our intuition and inner guidance is strong and wise. We follow our own path with a deep knowing. The night sky fades and reveals the last bridge, the purple bridge.

We step onto it, enveloped by purple light. It flows into our crown chakra at the top of our head, opening our senses to higher wisdom and a connection to all there is. The purple light transmutes everything which detaches us from connecting to our own spirit-self and higher knowing. We are wise and share our wisdom with others freely.

The purple light now travels down to our third eye, throat chakra, heart chakra, solar plexus chakra, sacral chakra, root chakra and all the way into our Earth, anchoring our higher wisdom into our physical self.

We feel balanced, clear of all blocks and anything which doesn't serve us.

We notice the golden gate we came through at the beginning. We walk towards it and the golden light emanating from it creates a beautiful bubble of golden light around us, protecting us from all energies which do not serve us as we go about our day or during our sleep.

We step back through the golden gate. Our chakras are clear and bright. We thank the rainbow guard. He smiles and asks us to take deep breaths in and out. With each breath we become more and more aware of our physical body and surroundings. We feel lighter and brighter. We feel loved and safe. We feel wonderful. And so it is.

◆ ◆ ◆

ABOUT THE AUTHOR

Diana White

Books are simply magic. As soon as you open a book you are transported into another world, without ever having to leave your chair or sofa. Your imagination can be free and lead you wherever you wish to go. No passport or permission necessary.

I have always been a bookworm from a young age and have a keen interest in books about magic, sci-fi and adventures. I also loved reading and reciting poetry with my grandmother. She was always on hand to share her wisdom and help me with my reading.

Not much has changed now.
Never in a million years however would I have imagined writing my own books.... but here we are, I have done it.

After writing down poetry now and again my writing really kick-started in 2019. I had left a career as a fitness instructor due to problems with my back and suddenly I found my head filled with stories to write.

I wrote everything down which came to mind without ever thinking of becoming an author. I simply knew some day I would do something with it.

Apart from writing you can often find me outdoors as I'm a keen walker and nature lover.

I'm also a Psychic Medium and, considering my deep interest in magic and sci-fi which started in my childhood, I am not surprised I have taken this path too. It brings with it great responsibility but also provides a lot of love and healing to people.

You can find me on social media too:
Facebook: @mediumdiananwhite
Instagram: @mediumdianawhite

See you there.
With love,
Di

BOOKS BY THIS AUTHOR

Strawberry Witch

Matilda, the strawberry witch, loves nothing more than adventures, strawberries and her grandmother.

Meet Matilda and join her on 12 magical adventures. She is a true adventurer and loves to learn.

This book is suitable for children aged 4+ and a wonderful addition to bedtime stories or for anyone who is learning to read.

BOOKS BY THIS AUTHOR

Crystal's Journey Over The Rainbow

Crystal has always wondered what the rainbow is all about. She takes the plunge into the unknown and with that allows for some amazing discoveries about herself and life.

Each chapter is a colour of the rainbow which represents a different journey, guided by our chakras.

It helps us as individuals to understand each chakra, the importance of them, and also that life is a journey of discoveries including who we are as a person.

This book is suitable for children and adults alike.

Matilda

STRAWBERRY WITCH

Matilda loves nothing more than adventures, strawberries and her grandmother.

written and illustrated by Diana White

Crystal's journey over the rainbow

A journey of discovery and enlightenment

WRITTEN AND ILLUSTRATED BY
DIANA WHITE

Printed in Great Britain
by Amazon